CONT[ENTS]

Map references are denoted in the text b: ❶ Greater Boston ❷ Downtown Boston ❸ Harvard Square ❹ Downtown & Beacon Hill ❺ Boston Transit

boston places to see

Set in its ways and steeped in history, the city that gave birth to a nation is also young, vibrant, and ethnically mixed, home to a thriving arts community, classic architecture, a world-class symphony orchestra, outstanding higher education and medical institutions, and inhabitants who are sports and politics obsessed. Whether you're weaving through the narrow cobblestoned streets of the Freedom Trail, plunging into the Charles River aboard an amphibious landing craft, or downing chocolate martinis atop the Pru Center, you'll find a Boston where old embraces new and echoes of the country's struggle for liberty and independence go hand-in-hand with the color and hubbub of 21st-century street-performers, outdoor cafés, restaurants, and beautiful boutiques.

see it places to see

Sights

Arnold Arboretum ❷ 5C

With 15,000 specimens including beech, lilac, tulip, honeysuckle, and rarities from all around the world, Arnold Arboretum is one of the most proliferate tree collections in North America. Covering 265 acres and offering stunning views of Boston and the sea, this park is just one link in Boston's nine-mile-long 'Emerald Necklace' of public parks, planted by visionary landscape architect Frederick Law Olmsted in the 1880s. It's a rambling, picnicking, and painting paradise, with glorious displays all year round, from the

Glorious colors at the Arnold Arboretum

Cobblestoned Acorn Street in Beacon Hill

heady scent of 250 varieties of lilac in spring (for Lilac Sunday, *see p.60*) to the sea of gold produced by 130 kinds of maple in the fall. *Free adm. Open daily sunrise-sunset. www.arboretum.harvard.edu*

Back Bay & Newbury St ❷ 4D

It's hard to believe this sophisticated residential and fashion shopping nexus sprang out of mudflats in the 1850s. Today it's one of Boston's most elegant enclaves, with **Newbury** (*see p.20*) and **Boylston Streets** housing exclusive style-temples, galleries, jewelers, sidewalk cafés, and restaurants. Architecture buffs can enjoy a banquet of another kind at Copley Square, home to **Trinity Church** (a Neo-Romanesque extravaganza dating from 1877 and now ranked one of the top ten public buildings in the nation), and the **Boston Public Library**, a McKim, Mead & White mock-Renaissance building dating from 1887, decorated with murals by Sargent and Puvis de Chevannes, and statues by Gutzon Borglum, sculptor of Mount Rushmore. *Free art &*

architecture tours Sun 2pm (Oct-May), Mon 2.30pm, Tue, Thu 6pm, Fri, Sat 11am, Boston Public Library, Copley Sq, T: 617 536 5400, www.bpl.org

Beacon Hill & Cheers Bar ❷ 3E

Beacon Hill is quintessential Boston: historic, posh, and picturesque, with some of the finest Federal architecture in the country. Furnished with gas lights and pretty wrought-iron fencing, its quaint, brick-laid sidewalks make ideal strolling terrain: highlights include the 1.6-mile **Black Heritage Trail** (see 'Behind Closed Doors', p.14), the cobblestoned **Acorn St**, and **Louisburg Sq** (the only private square in Boston), the **Nicholls House**, epitome of 19th-century gentility, and the **Harrison Gray Otis House** (see p.59) built by Charles Bulfinch, architect of Washington's Capitol, in 1796.

For lunch or coffee, seek out **Charles St** with its smart cafés, restaurants, and food stores, or enjoy a pint at **Cheers** (see p.47), model for the bar in the legendary TV series and now a tourist shrine in its own right.

Boston Common ❷ 4E & ❹

Established in 1634 as a 'trayning ground' for the colonial militia and also 'for the feeding of Cattell', Boston Common is the oldest public park in North America: Quakers and witches were hanged here in the 17th century, its cemetery contains the graves of families from the Boston Tea Party, and in 1776 British Redcoats used it as their camp HQ. Cows were outlawed in 1830 and the 48-acre common is now a place

Sunshine and tulips on Boston Common

for promenading, picnicking, and walking dogs, skating on Frog Pond, and frisbee throwing. *Open daily. 146 Tremont St, T: 617 426 3115.*

Faneuil Hall Marketplace ❷ 3G & ❹

Aka the 'Cradle of Liberty', Faneuil Hall, which is pronounced 'Fan-yull', 'Fan-ull', or even 'Fan-you-al', was where opposition to British rule

Quack Cousteau

For the ultimate Boston experience, take a 'duck' ride in a World War II amphibious landing vehicle through Back Bay, Beacon Hill, and North End to Charlestown for an 80-minute cruise along the Charles River. Tickets must be purchased on the web or up to five days in advance from Pru Center. *Open daily Apr-Dec 9am-sunset, departs Pru Center (❷ 5C) or Museum of Science (❷ 2E); T: 617 267 3825, www.bostonducktours.com*

5

The elaborate dome of Faneuil Hall

detonated from the 1760s onwards. Samuel Adams and his fellow patriots often met and debated here; subsequent speakers in the historic hall have included Daniel Webster and Frederick Douglass, Susan Anthony, Martin Luther King, JFK, Desmond Tutu, and the Dalai Lama. Today Park Rangers stage mock Revolutionary debates in the second-floor meeting hall. In the 1970s, Faneuil Hall and the Marketplace were converted into a lively shopping center with professional street entertainers, unusual souvenir shops, big-name retailers, top-notch Yankee restaurants, and an exotic food court. *15 State St at Congress, T: 617 523 1300.*

Fenway Park ❷ 4A

Fenway Park is Boston's hallowed 'field of dreams' and a mecca for baseball fans across the globe. Opened in April 1912, the park has seen incredible performances by hall-of-famers Babe Ruth, Ted Williams (who hit 406 here in 1941), Carl Yastrzemski, and Carlton Fisk. It's the oldest-running Major League ballpark in the nation and with just 33,871 seats packed into a tiny 10-acre lot, it's also one of the quirkiest, notorious for its angles and the infamous 'Green Monster',

Rags and Riches

Best known for his dollar-bill portraits of George Washington, Gilbert Stuart is buried in Tomb 61, a pauper's grave in Boston Common's Central Burying Ground (❷ 4E). Other luminaries in the same graveyard include revolutionary soldiers, British Redcoats, and some of the organisers of the Boston Tea Party.

a giant wall built in 1936 to shield overlooking windows. Catch a game (see p. 36), or take a guided tour *Daily 9am-4pm, tours leave from the Souvenir Store across Yawkey Way, T: 617 226 6666, www.redsox.com*

The great Fenway Park stadium

The Freedom Trail ❷ 4F-1H

Starting out from Boston Common (see p.5 and red dotted line on map ❷), and stopping off at places where the first American patriots lived and fought for modern liberty, the Freedom Trail provides insight into historic Boston. A 2.5-mile red-brick path weaves through three neighborhoods taking in 16 important sites, including churches, cemeteries, and architecture more than two centuries old. Allow three to four hours for a leisurely stroll or take the two-hour self-controlled audio tour (Apr-Nov). Costumed actors lead tours from the **Boston Common Visitor Center** (147 Tremont St, T: 617 357 8300) and Bostix Booth at Faneuil Hall Marketplace on a variety of themes including the Freedom Trail, historic pubs, and Boston's port.
www.thefreedomtrail.org

Harvard Square ❶ 4C & ❸

With its funky shops, pubs, clubs, lively café scene, and elegant restaurants, Harvard Square represents the hub of Cambridge,

Costumed guards march the Freedom Trail

where anybody and everybody congregates, particularly by the entrance to the subway – aka 'the Pit': people-watchers, students, chess players, buskers, tourists, skate-punks, and mavericks galore. Browse through the abundance of bookshops (specialties range from poetry to Japanese arcana), play chess outside Holyoke Center, buy a gourmet picnic at Cardullo's (see p.25) or

enjoy some of the world's most talented musicians, magicians, and street performers over an ice cream from Toscanini's (see 'Scooper Dooper', p.42). Close by are the quads of Harvard Yard, the tree-shaded inner sanctum of the powerhouse that has churned out six presidents, 11 Supreme Court justices, and 30 Nobel Laureates. Student guided campus tours leave Mon-Sat: twice a day during the academic year and

Chess challenge in Harvard Square

Discount Admission

Many of Boston's museums host free or discount sessions: the Museum of Fine Arts (*see p.10*) asks for a contribution Wednesday 4-9.45pm, the Harvard Natural History and Peabody Museums (*see right*) are free Sunday until 12pm and Wednesday 3-5pm September to May. Harvard Art Museums (❶ 4C) is free Saturday until 12pm. The Children's Museum (*see p.60*) charges $1 Friday 5-9pm.

four times a day in the summer from Holyoke Center - phone ahead.
T: 800 862 5678, www.cambridge-usa.org, www.harvardsquare.com

Harvard University Museums ❶ 4C & ❸

With an awesome collection of art, the university museums cover the blocks east and north of Harvard Yard. **The Museum of Natural History** contains an astonishing collection of 3,000 glass flowers, handblown from 1887-1936 in Germany; the **Peabody Museum** houses more than a million archeological artifacts from gold and textiles to totem poles and Easter Island effigies. As for art, Harvard eclipses most public collections with the outstanding **Fogg**, spanning medieval art, American landscape, the Pre-Raphaelites, and the French Impressionists. The **Sackler** is devoted to Asian, Islamic, and Indian cultures; and the **Busch Reisinger** has one of the best hauls of German 20th-century art anywhere. *Adm to one art gallery includes entrance to the others; entrance to the Museum of Natural History includes the Peabody and vice versa; alternatively purchase a Harvard Hot Ticket, good for entrance to all six museums for just $10.* HMNH: 26 Oxford St, T: 617 495 3045, www.hmnh.harvard.edu; **Museums:** Adm. 32 Quincy St, T; 617 495 3045, www.artmuseums.harvard.edu

Institute of Contemporary Art ❷ 4B

Founded in 1936, Boston ICA was the first US art institution to welcome artists fleeing Nazi Europe,

Glass flowers, Museum of Natural History

and also the first to exhibit Gauguin, Munch, Schiele, Kokoschka, and Picasso's *Guernica*. In Sepptember 2006 the collection re-opens in a stunning new building at Fan Pier; its dramatic façade harbors a glass-walled theater, restaurant, and gallery and it is now Boston's premier contemporary art venue. *100 Northern Ave, T: 617 266 5152, www.icaboston.org*

Isabella Stewart Gardner Museum ❷ 5A

An exquisite private collection, packed with treasures and unchanged since Isabella Stewart Gardner's death in 1924. A wealthy socialite and ardent Red Sox fan (*see pp.6, 36*), Mrs Gardner modeled the museum on a Venetian-style palazzo, building a spectacular three-story garden courtyard in the center and filling it with flowers, ferns, and light. Around the courtyard are artifacts spanning 30 centuries of culture, from Renaissance altarpieces and 17th-century tapestries to works by Fra Angelico, Matisse, and Whistler. It also includes Sargent's

Boston City Pass

Valid for nine days and costing $39 ($21.25 for kids aged three-11), the Boston City Pass saves 50 per cent on the total cost of visiting the following attractions: the New England Aquarium (*see p.12*), the Museum of Fine Arts (*see p.10*), the Museum of Science (*see p.11*), the Harvard Museum of Natural History (*see left*), the JFK Library & Museum (*see right*), and the Skywalk Observatory (*see box, below*). Purchase the pass direct from sights or online.
www.citypass.net

Portrait of Mrs Gardner, in which she is wearing a low-cut dress considered so shocking at the time it had to be withdrawn from the show. *Adm. Open Tue-Sun 11am-5pm, 280 The Fenway at Palace Rd, T: 617 566 1401, www.gardnermuseum.org*

John F Kennedy Museum & Library ❶ 5E

From its vantage point overlooking Boston Harbor and the downtown skyline, the John F Kennedy Museum & Library movingly commemorates the life and presidency of Boston's most famous icon. Housed in a monumental glass and concrete building by I M Pei, the museum evokes the period vividly, using a mixture of original footage, personal memorabilia, and recreations of the Oval Office to chronicle key events in the presidency. These include the 13-day Cuban Missile Crisis, the Nixon Debates, the civil rights debate, and the launch of the US Space Program. *Adm. Open daily*

Climb to the Sky

For 360° bird's-eye views of Boston, take the 50-story elevator ride to the Skywalk Observatory on top of the Prudential Center (❷4C). *800 Boylston St, T: 617 236 3100, www.prudentialcenter.com*

Massachusetts State House
❷ 3F & ❹

The glittering 23-carat gold dome of the State House is one of Boston's most eye-catching landmarks. This masterpiece was the work of Boston-born architect Charles Bulfinch, father of the Federal style and inspiration for capitol buildings across the nation. Its cornerstone was laid by Samuel Adams on 4 July 1795 and its dome was sheathed in copper rolled by Paul Revere. It is open to the public, although only US presidents and retiring governors can use the front door. Highlights of the interior include the Sacred Cod, hanging above the public gallery in the House of Representatives. This was donated by a merchant in 1783 to remind the legislature of the

Elegant façade of the Massachusetts State House

region's most important industry – fishing. *Adm and guided tours of the interior are free. Open Mon-Fri 10am-4pm. Beacon & Park Sts, T: 617 727 7030, www.sec.state.ma.us/trs/trsidx.htm*

Museum of Fine Arts (MFA) **❷ 5A**
The jewel in the crown of Boston's art museums, decorated with murals

Culture Combos
Combine art with music at Boston's top museums: at MFA (see below) there's courtyard Latin, jazz, and contemporary concerts in the summer (Wednesday 7.30pm) and jazz with cocktails all year round as well as live music on Fridays. At the Isabella Stewart Gardner Museum (see p.9) there are jazz and chamber music concerts in the Tapestry Room, on Sunday afternoons in spring and fall.
T: 617 278 5156 for schedules, www.gardnermuseum.org

by John Singer Sargent, containing more than one million works of art in a 16-acre site. Some galleries will be relocated by 2009, while the Art of Americas collection expands into a stunning new East Wing and Garden Courtyard by architect Norman Foster. Gallery collections range from Egyptian mummies, Nubian masks, and the largest collection of Asian art in the West, to American painting (including Gilbert Stuart's dollar bill portrait of Washington). As well as US folk art, there are Impressionist

The stupendous Museum of Fine Arts

Flying high in the Museum of Science

works by Manet, Cézanne, Degas, and Monet, plus paintings by Gauguin and Van Gogh. Check out summer Fridays, with live music in Calderwood Courtyard. *Adm includes guided tour. Open Sat-Tue 10am-4.45pm, Wed-Fri 10am-9.45pm. 465 Huntington Ave at Museum St, T: 617 267 9300, www.mfa.org*

Museum of Science ❷ 1E

From hatching chickens to 15-ft-long bolts of lightning, the Museum of Science brings science, natural history, medicine, dinosaurs, astronomy, biology, and physics to life with a mass of mind-blowing interactives and presentations. Must-sees include a state-of-the-art IMAX and Planetarium, chick hatchery, and the Thomson Theater of Electricity, used for staging 2.5m-volt lightning shows with the world's largest Van de Graaf generator. Kids can create virtual critters for the 1,700-sq-ft Virtual Fish Tank, and meet owls,

Cute little seal at the New England Aquarium

skinks, porcupines, and other animals. Adults should visit Friday evening, for cocktails and appetizers at the Science St Café and stargazing at the Gilliland Observatory. Book in advance. *Adm. Open 9am-5pm daily, till 9pm Fri, and till 7pm July 5-Labor Day (1st Mon Sept). Science Park btw Storough & Memorial Drives, T: 617 723 2500, www.mos.org*

New England Aquarium ❷4H

The New England Aquarium is home to 25,000 animals from 500 species, including sea lions, otters, stingrays, barracuda, sharks, and Myrtle the Sea Turtle. In the awesome 200,000-gallon, four-story-high cylindrical Giant Ocean Tank, visitors can get as close up to a coral reef as real deep-sea divers. Around it, the impressive Penguin Pool houses rockhopper, jackass, and dwarf blue penguins from Australasia (only 12 inches high

Call Me Ishmael

For the boat trip of a lifetime, leave the skyscrapers behind and head off to see the largest animals that roam the earth. Watch the humpback whales frolicking in the waters of their summer feeding-grounds at Stellwagen Marine Sanctuary. Whale-watching trips take three to four hours, tickets $32.55. *Open Apr-Oct, New England Aquarium (❷4H), T: 617 973 5200, www.neaq.org*

and weighing two pounds). Other highlights include the working animal hospital and an IMAX theater where a gigantic screen lets audiences dive into coral reefs without getting wet. *Open 9am-5pm daily & till 6pm weekends, Central Wharf at Atlantic Ave & Milk St, T: 617 973 5200, www.neaq.org*

North End & Paul Revere House ❷3H

From the Puritans onwards, North End has been settled by immigrants: Irish, Jewish East Europeans, the Portuguese in the 19th century, and

Paul Revere on horseback bound for Lexington

Best Free Sights

Boston has masses of fabulous free sights, including Boston Public Library (**2**4C) for art and architecture tours, Trinity Church (**2**4D) for Friday organ recitals (*12.15pm, Sep-Jun, www.trinityboston.org*), and the Holocaust Memorial (Union St at Congress, **2**3G). The *USS Constitution* (*see p.15*) offers free tours, the Esplanade (**2**3A-2F) is a jogging, sun-bathing, and inline skating paradise with free concerts at the Hatch Shell June through October. Finally, Bunker Hill Monument (**2**1G) is a 291-ft obelisk perched above Boston Harbor with free Park Ranger talks on details of the battle on nearby Breed's Hill.

southern Italians from 1910. Though increasingly gentrified, it's still a stubbornly Italian, 'Godfather'-ish neighborhood with laundry-draggled balconies; on Hanover and Salem Sts a cluster of coffee houses, *trattorie*, and pastry shops tempt passers-by with coffee, cannoli, tiramisu, and homemade ice cream. Historic sights include the **Paul Revere House**, built in 1680 and home to Revere's 16 children as well as the starting place for his famous 15-mile midnight ride to Lexington. There is also beautiful **Old North Church**, built after a church by Wren with box-pews and a needle-thin steeple, and the atmospheric **Copp's Hill Burying Ground** with its stunning views of Boston Harbor and tombstones dating back to 1659. Paul Revere House: *Adm. Open daily 9.30am-5.15pm (Nov-Apr 4.15pm), 19 North Sq, T: 617 523 2338, www.paulreverehouse.org*

Behind Closed Doors

Starting out from the Shaw Memorial on Beacon St (**2** 4F and *purple dotted line on map* **2**), the 1.6-mile Black Heritage Trail tells the story of the African Americans in Boston. It covers the arrival of the slaves in 1638 through to the establishment of the first interracial schools and churches in the 19th century. *Open Mon-Sat 10am-4pm, T: 617 725 0022, www.afroammuseum.org; daily guided tours are run Jun-Aug, T: 617 742 5415.*

Old State House Museum
2 4G & cover map

Still holding its own in a thicket of 20th-century glass-walled skyscrapers, the imposing Old State House was the hub of colonial administration from 1713. The merchant exchange soon became a hotbed of rebellion and a circle of cobblestones outside commemorates the Boston Massacre

of 1770, when British soldiers fired on a defiant mob, killing five Bostonians. Six years later, on 18 July 1776, the Declaration of Independence was read from the balcony, followed by the symbolic burning of the Lion and Unicorn flag. A museum inside chronicles the history, with artifacts including John Hancock's frockcoat, Revere's (*see p.12*) engraving of the massacre, and tea from the world-famous

Take a break on a swan in the Public Garden

party. *Adm. Open daily 9am-5pm, longer in summer. 206 Washington St at State St, T: 617 720 1713, www.bostonhistory.org*

The Public Garden **2** 4E

No trip to the city is complete without a glide along the Public Garden lagoon in one of Boston's idyllic Swan Boats, inspired by the Wagner opera *Lohengrin*, owned by the Paget family since 1877 and

Harbor Islands

Left behind by glaciers in the Ice Age, the Harbor Islands and their wild tracts of shorebirds, swimming beaches, wild flowers, clifftops, winding trails, rolling hills, and salt marshes are a world apart. Six of the 31 islands are open to the public from May to October: to get there take a ferry from Long Wharf (❷ 4H, by New England Aquarium, *see p.12*) to George's Island. Water-taxis take passengers to Gallop's, Lovell's, Peddock's, Bumpkin, and Grape islands. Get info from the kiosk on Long Wharf, T: 617 223 8666, www.bostonislands.com

originally constructed out of wood, copper, and bicycle parts. The Public Garden dates back further still to 1837, when it was sculpted out of landfill to become the first botanical garden in the US. In among the beautifully kept beds and lawns are 125 types of tree, including cork, sequoia, and giant Manchurian redwood; statues range from George Washington to the cute Jack, Kack, Mack, Nack, Quack, and Pack from Robert McCloskey's 1941 children's story *Make Way for Ducklings*.
Swan Boats: www.swanboats.com

USS Constitution ❷ 1H

Launched in 1797, 'Old Ironsides' saw nearly a century of undefeated service, winning 42 engagements. With her 52 guns and six anchors, the grand old war-horse got her nickname in 1812, when cannon balls bounced off her sides, inducing British sailors to cry out 'Huzzah! Her sides are made of iron!' In fact they were made of three layers of live oak, a resilient and rot-proof species unique to America. The ship is the oldest fully commissioned vessel in the world and the flagship of the US Navy: sailors take visitors on 30-minute guided tours (*see 'Best Free Sights', p.13*) and fire its cannon daily. Open Tue-Sun 10am-5.50pm Apr-Oct, Thu-Sun 10am-3.50pm Nov-Mar. Long Wharf, Charlestown, T: 617 242 7511, www.ussconstitution.navy.mil

Old Ironsides herself – the USS Constitution

15

The stunning Boston waterfront illuminated at twilight.

boston places to shop

Museum-quality antiques or modern design classics, art deco china or elaborate rhinestone jewelry, used and rare books, New England delicacies or funky knick-knacks, department-store ritz or a pound of clothing for a dollar – Boston has something to tempt every shopper. And with no sales tax on clothing and just five per cent on other goods, value for money is guaranteed. Start your shopping spree in Faneuil Hall or Downtown Crossing, then take the T to elegant Newbury Street or Harvard Square for boutiques and bookstores galore.

buy it places to shop

Top Shopping Strips

Charles St ❷ 3E

Patronised by the well-groomed of Boston, exclusive Charles Street is Beacon Hill's main shopping area: come here for antiques, exclusive gifts, homeware shops, and chic, expensive fashion boutiques, as well as gourmet grocers.

Elegant shops along Newbury Street

Newbury St ❷ 4B–4D

Eight-block stretch of retail heaven, jammed with spas, bars, art galleries, and snazzy fashion joints, from smart designer flagships (Christian Dior, Agnes B, Armani, Hermès, Brooks Brothers, and Kate Spade) to the excruciatingly flash Louis Boston (*see p.24*). The fashion beat gets funkier the closer you get to Mass Ave and Kenmore Sq (❷4A); for thickets of easy-access chain stores don't miss the malls at Copley Place (❷5D) and Pru Center (❷4C).

Harvard Sq ❶ 4C & ❸

A dense concentration of specialty bookstores and shops for high fashion or retro chic, smart homeware, and furniture. The mood gets cooler and more student-oriented towards Central Sq and Davis Sq (❶4D) in Somerville, a gentrified mix of hip boutiques, offbeat giftshops, cafés, restaurants, antiques, thrift, and used CD stores.

Downtown Crossing ❷4F & ❹

The jewel in the crown of this

Old-Time Boston
For a quality selection of authentic Boston memorabilia, don't miss the old-fashioned toys, ornaments, jewelry, pewter, oil lamps, and lobster-print tea towels at Faneuil Hall Heritage Gift Shop (❷4G), in the basement of Faneuil Hall, *Stall 13, Faneuil Hall Sq, T: 617 723 1776.*

pedestrian shopping mall is Macy's (*see p.23*), a veritable shrine for shopaholic's. There's also a plethora of big chain stores, discount clothes, and shoe outlets, and Brattle Book Shop (*see p.22*), the oldest in the nation.

Faneuil Hall
Marketplace ❷ 3G & ❹

With its boutiques, gift stores, restaurants, and food stalls, the converted 19th-century market buildings of Faneuil Hall are touristy but fun, with cobblestone courtyards and an army of street performers.

South End ❷ 5C

Separated from Back Bay by Copley Place shopping mall, the colourful communities of South End host a vibrant, eclectic mix of shops, restaurants, and jazz clubs, clustered for the most part along the arteries of Tremont St and Columbus Ave (❷5D-6D).

Antiques

The Boston Antique
Co-operative ❷ 3E

International antiques from the 16th to the 20th century with a focus on 18th-century European furniture. *119 Charles St, T: 617 224 9811, www.bostonantiqueco-op.com*

Elegant Findings ❷ 3E

A fabulous selection of Meissen porcelain, antique linens, and also furniture. *89 Charles St btw Pinckney & Mt Vernon, T: 617 973 4844.*

India Antiques, Art, & Music ❷ 4C

Glittering with goodies from every part of India: beautiful antique religious statuary, pashminas, henna tattoos, brightly colored gold jewelry, and musical instruments. *279 Newbury St at Gloucester St, T: 617 266 6539*

Judith Dowling Asian Art
& Antiques ❷ 3E

Priceless Japanese, Chinese, and Korean art. *133 Charles St btw Phillips & Revere Sts, T: 617 523 5211.*

Machine Age ❷ 6G

Facing the waterfront, Machine Age's new showrooms stock 20th-century design classics, vintage and modern, with superb furniture by Eames, Knoll, and Dunbar; also collectibles, paintings, and props. *645 Summer St at A St, T: 617 482 0048, www.machine-age.com*

Unique Boutiques

Whether you're looking for a luminous chess set, a William Morris rug, or a miniature Van de Graaf generator, Boston is home to a wealth of museum boutiques. Seek out the MFA (*see p.10*) for Eiffel Tower scarves and Nordic sweaters; the Museum of Science (*see p.11*), for space chess, anti-gravity globes, and astronaut ice cream. The Gardner (*see p.9*) is unbeatable for delicate silk scarves and pretty imported Italian ceramics; and MIT Museum (❷ 1B) is the premier outlet for delights like moon-walker robots and rocket-cars powered by baking soda and vinegar.

Twentieth Century Ltd ● 3E

This shop specializes in highly desirable (and often extremely expensive) 20th-century Americana – from art deco china to beautiful and brightly colored 1960s' rhinestone jewelry. *73 Charles St btw Pinckney & Mt Vernon Sts, T: 617 742 1031.*

Art Supplies

Pearl Art & Craft Supplies ● 4C

Monster discount art store on three floors and bursting with bargains. *579 Mass Ave btw Essex & Pearl Sts, Cambridge, T: 617 547 6600, www.pearlpaint.com*

Bookstores

With its mass of new, used, and quirky specialty bookstores, Boston is a bookworm's heaven.

Brattle Book Shop ● 4F

Sift through the $-racks outside or trawl through three levels of secondhand books at this haven dating back to 1825. *9 West St, Downtown Crossing, T: 617 542 0210, www.brattlebookshop.com*

Brookline Booksmith ● 4C

Independent bookseller and a top venue for book readings and talks. *279 Harvard St at Coolidge Corner, Brookline Sts, T: 617 566 6660, www.brooklinebooksmith.com*

Comicopia ● 2H

A must for comic-book fans, this store stocks old favourites as well as underground hits. And with several thousand comic paperbacks to sift through you're bound to find something you like. *464 Commercial Ave, Kenmore Square, T: 617 266 4266, www.comicopia.com*

Grolier Poetry Book Shop ● 4C

This literary beacon with more than 14,000 volumes of poetry awards a prestigious annual poetry prize. *6 Plympton St at Mass Ave, Harvard Sq, Cambridge, T: 617 547 4648, www.grolierpoetrybookshop.com*

Harvard Book Store ● 4C

New, used, and remaindered high-brow titles. Rub shoulders with authors and the intelligentsia who read them. Literary events are held in the bookshop. *Open daily Fri till 10pm, Sat 12 am, 1256 Mass Ave at Harvard University, Cambridge, T: 800 542 7323, www.harvard.com*

Kate's Mystery Books ❶ 3C

Limitless supplies of mystery fiction, with author-signings by celeb writers John Katzenbach, Robert Parker, and Elmore Leonard. *2211 Mass Ave at Day St nr Davis Sq, T: 617 491 2660, www.katesmysterybooks.com*

MIT Press Bookstore ❷ 2C

There's no ducking under it, this is high-brow and proud of it. Go in search of a modern enlightenment; you may be surprised. *Open daily to 7pm (6pm on weekends and 8.30pm on Thu). 292 Main St, Kendall Square, T: 617 253 5249, mitpress.mit.edu/bookstore*

Department Stores

Lord and Taylor ❷ 4C

Small-scale and manageable, with a choice selection of classic American designer men's, women's, and kid's clothing as well as shoes, jewelry, and cosmetics. *760 Boylston St at Exeter St, T: 617 262 6000, www.lordandtaylor.com*

Hang around for the designer bargains

Macy's ❷ 4F & ❹

Boston's oldest department store (founded as Filene's in 1881) is still recognisable by its elaborate Beaux Arts façade, though it converted to a Macy's in 2006. It is renowned for bridal gowns but the store also sells fashion, home furnishings, garden tools, cosmetics, and so on, and has one of the city's biggest and best bargain basements. *450 Washington St at Summer St, Downtown Crossing, T: 617 357 3000, www.macys.com*

Neiman Marcus ❷ 5C

Boston's glitziest department store: three floors of designer clothing, jewelry, and shoes to die for. *5 Copley Pl at Boylston St, T: 617 536 3660, www.neimanmarcus.com*

Saks Fifth Avenue ❷ 4C

Fifth Avenue glamour, with all the big names and some younger and fresher designer labels. Also shoes, jewelry, and cosmetics. *Prudential Plaza, T: 617 262 8500, www.saksfifthavenue.com*

Designer Shops

Alan Bilzerian ❷ 4D

Euro-*haute couture*: Dior, Ann Demeulemeester, Gaultier, Galliano, Jipijapa, Comme des Garçons, with essential clubwear in the basement. *34 Newbury St btw Arlington & Berkeley Sts, T: 617 536 1001, www.alanbilzerian.com*

Allston Beat ❷ 4B

Riotous, funky hipster's haven selling the complete spectrum of clubgear: from rubber, shiny vinyl, and fake fur to body jewelry and Doc Martens. *348 Newbury St btw Hereford St & Mass Ave, T: 617 421 9555.*

American Apparel ❷ 4D

This LA company has a positive anti-sweatshop stance and beautiful, wearable clothes for adults and kids. *138 Newbury St, T: 617 536 4768, www.americanapparel.net*

Brooks Brothers ❷ 4D

Shirtfronts don't get crisper than at this arbiter of good taste. *46 Newbury St at Berkeley St, T: 617 267 2600.*

Louis Boston ❷ 4D

The *ne plus ultra* of Bostonian *couture*: here are four floors of top international men's and women's designers (Lang, Lauren, Sander) in a superb Victorian building that was originally the city's Museum of Natural History. Take in the glitz and ritz over an espresso in the chic store café, which is practically a Boston institution in itself. *234 Berkeley St at Newbury, T: 800 225 1535, www.louisboston.com*

Riccardi ❷ 4D

'Just discovered' Euro designerwear alongside more established labels: Westwood, Comme des Garçons, Romeo Gigli, Prada, Miu Miu, Thierry Mugler, and Dolce & Gabbana. *116 Newbury St btw Clarendon & Dartmouth Sts, T: 617 266 3158, www.riccardiboston.com*

Wish ❷ 3E

Fun but foxy women's clothes, expensive and irresistible. *49 Charles St btw Mt Vernon & Chestnut St, T: 617 227 4441.*

Design Discount

The Closet ❷ 4C

Designer-chic resale for both sexes. *175 Newbury St btw Dartmouth & Exeter Sts, T: 617 536 1919.*

Wrentham Village Off map

130 designer discount outlets, 20

Quality shines through at Louis Boston

minutes out of town. *1 Premium Outlets Blvd, Wrentham, T: 508 384 0600, www.outletsonline.com*

Second Time Around Collections ❷ 4C

A fabulous treasure-trove of used, vintage and consignment designer clothes for men and women. *176 Newbury St btw Dartmouth & Exeter Sts, T: 617 247 3504*

Gourmet Food

Bakeries

North End has some of the best Italian bakeries in the world. For tasty, fresh, oven bread and pizza check out **Bova's** (❷3G, *open 24 hours at 134 Salem St at Prince St, T: 617 523 5601*), **Mike's** for yummy cakes and cannoli (❷3G, *300 Hanover St, T: 617 742 3050*), and **Modern Pastry Shop** for nougat and florentines (❷3G, *257 Hanover St btw Cross & Richmond Sts, T: 617 523 3783*).

Enticing cake counter at Mike's

Cardullo's Gourmet Shoppe ❶4C
Fine foods, beverages, and a mouth-watering delicatessen, plus a fantastic range of New England delicacies including Boston baked beans, Vermont maple syrup, and chocolate lobsters. *6 Brattle St at JFK St, Cambridge, T: 617 491 8888, www.cardullos.com*

South End Formaggio ❷6D
Cheese nirvana, with more than 250 rare varieties from Brie to Vermont goat's-milk feta, also homemade pastas and soups, coffee,

The window of Cardullo's Gourmet Shoppe

wines, olives, and cookies. *268 Shawmut Ave at Hanson St, T: 617 350 6996.*

DeLuca's Market ❷4C
Charming, old-style gourmet market, crammed with fancy foodstuffs, from outstanding homemade sandwiches to fruits, vegetables, deli, wines, and beers. *229 Newbury St at Fairfield, T: 617 262 5990.* **Branch:** *11 Charles St, Beacon Hill, T: 617 523 4343, www.delucasmarket.com*

Rosie's Bakery ❶4C
Purveyor of Boston's ultimate, much-adored fudge brownie: rich, brown, and wicked. *243 Hampshire St, Inman Sq, Cambridge, T: 617 491 9488, www.rosiesbakery.com*

Salumeria Italiana ❷3H
Superlative Neapolitan deli serving olive oils, balsamic vinegars, cheeses, biscuits, pasta, breads, olives, antipasti, and everything you need for a truly hedonistic gourmet picnic. *151 Richmond St btw Hanover & North Sts, T: 800 400 5916.*

Savenor's ❶ 3E

Connoisseur's cheeses, deli, and meats, perfect for picnics on Charles River Esplanade. *160 Charles St at Cambridge St, T: 617 723 6328.*

Specialty Shops

Abodeon ❶ 4C

A trove of retro chic – whether it's go-go boots, fondue sets, snow domes, vintage TVs, or oliblocks, Abodeon will come up trumps. *1731 Mass Ave at Garfield St, Cambridge, T: 617 497 0137.*

Beadworks ❷ 4C

Hundreds and thousands of beads from every part of the world and in every conceivable size and shape. *167 Newbury St btw Dartmouth & Exeter St, T: 617 247 7227.*

Black Ink ❷ 3E

Fun and funky knick-knacks: rubber stamps, ribbons, magnets, children's books, Tintin paraphernalia, and juicers. *101 Charles St at Pinckney St, T: 617 723 3883.*

Farmers' Markets

From May to November taste and buy locally grown produce – succulent peaches, fresh corn, blueberries, maple syrup, honey, cheese, and breads – at the Farmers' Markets in Copley Sq & St James Ave (❷4D) *Tue & Fri 11am-6pm,* and City Hall Plaza (❸3G), *Mon & Wed 11am-6pm, T: 781 893 8222, www.massfarmersmarkets.org*

Gloucester Street Cigar Company ❷ 4B

One of the largest humidors in Boston. Sells 180 kinds of cigars and 200 varieties of tobacco, plus loads of smoking accessories. *34 Gloucester St at Newbury, T: 617 424 1000, www.gstreetcigar.com*

Curious George Goes to Wordsworth ❶ 4C

Treasure chest of more than 20,000 children's book titles, from classics to activity, with kid-friendly reading

huts, toys, and games including stuffed animals and firemen's hats. *1 JFK St, Harvard Sq, T: 617 498 0062.*

Jack's Joke Shop ❷ 4E

Established in 1922, this family-run joke shop has a bottomless supply of tricks and gags, not to mention 250 styles of wig and 300 masks. *226 Tremont & Washington Sts, T: 617 426 9640, www.jacksjokes.com*

Buy a picnic at DeLuca's Market

Joie de Vivre off map
A top choice for gifts with everything from novelty cruets to jewelry, clocks, pictures frames, and children's toys. *1792 Mass Ave, T: 617 864 8188.*

Harvard Coop ❶4C & cover map
Books and an MIT Museum Gift Shop outlet (*see box, p.21*). *1400 Mass Ave at Harvard Sq, T: 617 499 2000, www.thecoop.com*

Hounds on the Hill ❷3E
Haute couture for dogs and cats. *103 Charles St at Pinckney St, T: 617 723 3266.*

Koo de Kir ❷3E
Chic and funky 21st-century design: scoring stratospheric on trend quotient, with intriguing furnishings, tableware, rugs, jewelry, and gifts guaranteed to inflict an instant *coup de coeur.* *65 Chestnut St, T: 617 723 8111, www.koodekir.com*

Nuggets ❷4A
More than 40 years of second-hand jazz, rock, ska, and R&B CDs, vinyl, and tapes, also fanzines, posters, and a $1 bargain bin. *486 Commonwealth Ave at Kenmore St, T: 617 536 0679.*

Explore Curious George goes to Wordsworth

Vintage & Thrift

The Closet Upstairs ❷4C
Vintage gems in top condition – 1920s' flapper-girl prom dresses, Victorian wedding dresses, mad hats, crazy shoes, and contemporary classics. *223 Newbury St btw Exeter & Fairfield Sts, T: 617 267 5757.*

Garment District & Dollar-a-Pound Plus ❷1C
Set aside several hours for this mammoth storehouse crammed with restyled used clothing, new clothes, funky accessories, and weathered jeans. Downstairs is the awesome Dollar-a-Pound, with second-hand clothing and accessories at $1.50 a pound or 75¢ on Friday, and records at 50¢ a pound. *200 Broadway at Davis St, Kendall Sq, Cambridge, T: 617 876 5230.*

Oona's ❶4C
Cambridge mecca for elegant hand-me-downs from the Roaring Twenties to the Summer-of-Love Seventies. *1210 Mass Ave btw Quincy & Bow Sts, Harvard Sq, T: 617 491 2654.*

boston entertainment

Bostonians – together with the thousands of college students who crowd into the city every year – take their entertainment seriously, and whether it's opera, merengue, improvised comedy, drum 'n' bass, experimental theater, poetry slams, or belly dancing, the performing-arts scene is as riveting as it is diverse and exciting. As for music, from classics to pop via everything in between, Boston has it all. Look for in-depth listings and incisive reviews on film, art, theater, music, clubs, and pop into the Boston Phoenix, online at *www.bostonphoenix.com*. For big events, reserve your tickets via Ticketmaster, *T: 617 931 2000, www.ticketmaster.com*, or TeleCharge, *T: 800 432 7250, www.telecharge.com*

watch it entertainment

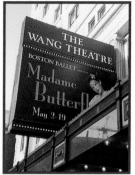
Musical at the Wang Center

Colonnaded entrance to the Boston Symphony Orchestra

Arts Center

Wang Center for the Performing Arts ❷ 5E

A magnificent 3,800-seat movie theater dating from 1925, now hosting a mix of Broadway-style plays, musical extravaganzas, and classic films, as well as the world-renowned Boston Ballet (*see p.32*). *270 Tremont St at Stuart St, T: 617 482 9393, www.wangcenter.org*

Classical Music

Boston is home to one of the best symphony orchestras on the planet and some of the finest music academies in the land.

Bank of America Celebrity Series

Debuts by internationally renowned artists – classical, modern, jazz, folk, and multi-media – various venues. The Celebrity Series has been entertaining since 1938. *T: 617 482 2595, www.celebrityseries.org*

Boston Lyric Opera ❷ 5E

Classic operas, world-class singers, and challenging interpretations. *Shubert Theater, 265 Tremont St at Stuart St, T: 800 447 7400, www.blo.org*

Boston Symphony Orchestra (BSO) ❷ 5B

An unmissable experience, with

Behind the Scenes at the Symphony

Take a free guided tour of the century-old Boston Symphony Hall (*see left*), considered one of the finest concert halls in the world. The hour-long tours are on Wednesday at 4.30pm and also the first Saturday of each month at 1.30pm between October-June: meet in the lobby of 301 Mass Ave (**2**5B) at *Huntington Ave, T: 617 638 9390, www.bso.org*

performances in the matchless Symphony Hall veering between perfect and sublime. The season runs from September-May, with Keith Lockhart's inimitable Boston Pops (*see box, right*) taking over May-mid July. *Symphony Hall, 301 Mass Ave at Huntington Ave, T: 617 266 1492, www.bso.org*

Handel & Haydn Society

One of the great Baroque orchestras led by top conductors including Christopher Hogwood. Various venues through the city, *T: 617 266 3605, www.handelandhaydn.org*

Isabella Stewart Gardner Museum **2**5A

Beautiful venue for concerts by jazz and string quartets (*see p.9*). Adm includes entrance to museum. *280 The Fenway at Palace Rd, T: 617 278 5156, www.gardnermuseum.org*

Jordan Hall **2**5B

Deluxe recitals by a mix of world-famous performers (Isaac Stern, Stan Getz, Benny Goodman, and Béla Bartók), the BSO Chamber Players, and the Boston Philharmonic under the charismatic baton of Benjamin Zander. *290 Huntington Ave at St Botolph St, T: 617 585 1100, www.newenglandconservatory.edu;* Boston Philharmonic: *see also www.bostonphil.org, T: 617 236 0999*

Museum of Fine Arts (MFA) **2**5A

A variety of music evenings where Baroque, Caribbean, and Tibetan sounds, outdoor Latin, jazz, Glenn Miller, and modern music provide the soundtrack. Check out the popular summer Fridays (*see box, p.10*). *465 Huntington Ave at Museum St, T: 617 369 3300, www.mfa.org*

Comedy

Comedy Connection **2**4G

Famous names and rising stars alike: with drinks and tasty appetizers. *245 Quincy Market Building, Faneuil Hall, T: 617 248 9700, www.comedyconnectionboston.com*

Tops of the Pops

The Boston Pops have been thrilling audiences with 'light music of the best class' since 1885. Today the Pops are the most recorded orchestra in the world: enjoy their innovative classical crossovers – world and folk music, dance, Glenn Miller, kd lang, and Elvis, at the Symphony Hall (**2**5B) *May-Jun and outdoors at the Hatch Shell (**2**3D) in Jul.*

Church Concerts

Boston's churches host a vibrant program of free or voluntary-donation recitals: highlights include noontime concerts on the 6,898-pipe organ at Trinity Church (❷4D), in Copley Sq, Fridays at 12.15pm, Sep-Jun. Bach cantatas are conducted by world-class names at Emmanuel Church (❷4D), 15 Newbury St at Berkeley St, on Sunday at 10am. For classical, jazz, and pop recitals, try King's Chapel (❷4F), corner of School & Tremont Sts at 12.15pm daily, Oct-May.

Comedy Studio ❶4C

Cambridge-based alternative comedy bastion and launchpad for new names. 1236 Mass Ave at Bow St, Cambridge, T: 617 661 6507, www.thecomedystudio.com

Improv Asylum ❷3H & 5E

Hilarious audience-suggested improvised comedy. Half-price tickets are sometimes available from BosTix (see box, right). 216 Hanover St at Prince St, and 75 Warrenton St at Charles Playhouse, T: 617 263 6887, www.improvasylum.com

Improv Boston ❶4C

As big on audience participation as it is on double entendre. Back Alley Theater, 1253 Cambridge St, T: 617 576 1253, www.improvboston.com

Dance

Boston Ballet ❷5E

One of the top dance companies in North America, with a wide-ranging repertoire. Wang Center (see p.30), 270 Tremont St at Stuart, T: 617 695 6950, www.bostonballet.org

Dance Clubs

Boston has three main nightclub strips: on Lansdowne St by Fenway Park (mainstream clubs, ❷4A), in the Theater District (❷4E-5F), and around Central Sq in Cambridge (❶4C). There are gay clubs in Back Bay (❷4D) and South End (❷6D)

Aria ❷5E

A sophisticated club of red velvet sofas, fashionable clientele and hip hop, R&B, reggae, and house. Jeans allowed for ladies only. 246 Tremont St, T: 617 338 7080, www.ariaboston.com

Avalon ❷4A

Huge and sweaty, with a 2,000 capacity, live bands, international DJs, and a mixed crowd for Friday night's Avaland. 15 Lansdowne St at Ipswich St, T: 617 262 2424, www.avalonboston.com

Axis ❷4A

On two floors with a mix of hard house, trance, progressive dance, and electronic music with forays into drag and strip. 13 Lansdowne St at Ipswich St, T: 617 262 2437.

The Big Easy ❷4E

Laidback New Orleans-style dance club with live bands, sofas, a private room, and techno sounds. *1 Boylston Pl btw Charles & Tremont Sts, T: 617 351 7000.*

Gypsy Bar ❷ 4C

Dress up to tuck into bistro cuisine before dancing the night away to local DJs. A popular local hangout. *116 Boylston St, T: 617 482 7799.*

La Boom ❷ 4E

Euro-chic, with lounge-club sofas and a mix of global house, hip-hop, and techno. *25 Boylston Pl btw Charles & Tremont Sts, T: 617 357 6800*

Phoenix Landing ❶ 4C

Quirky Irish dance club, with a dinner menu and Boston's grooviest trance music. *512 Mass Ave at Brookline St, Cambridge, T: 617 576 6260.*

The Roxy ❷ 4E

Multi-level former ballroom dishing up international house, techno, Top 40, and live music. *279 Tremont St at Stuart St, T: 617 338 7699.*

Salsa Boston ❶ 4D

Get your hips swinging at a hot,

Boston knows how to party

sexy, Latin evening with Salsa Boston who organise salsa nights, lessons and cruises. *T: 617 513 9841, www.salsaboston.com*

Jazz & Blues

Bob's Southern Bistro ❷ 6B

Live jazz and soul food all week and a Sunday jazz brunch. *604 Columbus Ave at Northampton St, T: 617 536 6204, www.bobthechef.com*

Regattabar ❶ 4C

Ultra-suave venue with top names in jazz and blues. Jazz festival in May.

Discount Tix

The BosTix Half-Price Tickets Outlet sells half-price, day-of-show tickets for theater, dance, and music events from 11am (cash only) from booths at Faneuil Hall (❷4G) and Copley Sq (❷4C). *Open Mon-Sat 10am-6pm, Sun 11am-4pm. See web site for daily listings: www.artsboston.org/bostix.cfm*

Charles Hotel, 1 Bennett St at Harvard Sq, Cambridge, T: 617 661 5000.

Ryles ❶ 4C

Salsa and merengue on Thurs, live music on Fri, and a tasty Sunday jazz brunch. *212 Hampshire St, Cambridge, T: 617 876 9330, www.rylesjazz.com*

Music to the Ears

Catch more than 600 free recitals, jazz, string quartets, and chamber music at the New England Conservatory's Jordan Hall (❷5A), *290 Huntington Ave at St Botolph St, T: 617 585 1100, www.newenglandconservatory.edu*

Sullers Jazz Club ❶4C

Listen to the likes of Harry Connick Jnr or Lou Rawls with serious jazz fans at this live music institution. DoubleTree Guest Suites Boston, 400 Soldiers Field Rd, 617 562 4111.

Wally's ❷6B

Boston's jazz cornerstone, a hole in the wall that has fostered legends in jazz. No cover charge. *427 Mass Ave at Columbus Ave, T: 617 424 1408.*

Rock & Pop

Cantab Lounge ❶4C

HQ to 1950s' rock & roll star Little

Outside the Paradise Rock

Joe Cook, featuring blues, bluegrass, local bands, and poetry slams. *738 Mass Ave at Inman St, Cambridge, T: 617 354 2685.*

Lizard Lounge ❶4C

Small, boho, no stage, and a mix of student and national bands. Poetry slams on Sunday, jazz on Monday. *1667 Mass Ave btw Harvard & Porter Sqs, Cambridge, T: 617 547 0759.*

Middle East ❶4C

The big hitter on Boston's alternative rock scene, with two large stages for hosting local and big-name bands, jazz, and acoustic music. With Middle-Eastern food and belly dancing. *472 Mass Ave at Central Sq, Cambridge, T: 617 864 EAST, www.mideastclub.com*

Orpheum ❷4F

Built in 1852 (it staged the premiere of Tchaikovsky's first piano concerto): now the hallowed stomping ground for aging rock stars. *1 Hamilton Place at Tremont St, T: 617 679 0810.*

Paradise Rock ❷3A

With two big spaces for rock, folk, jazz, and local grunge. *969 Commonwealth Ave at Babcock St, Brookline, T: 617 562 8800.*

TD Banknorth Garden ❷2G

Rock and pop concerts in a 19,600-seat arena. *One FleetCenter, Causeway St at Friend St, T: 617 931 2000, www.tdbanknorthgarden.com*

TT the Bear's Place ❶4C

Grungy live-music venue for homegrown punk and rock bands, plus bigger names. *10 Brookline St at Mass Ave, Cambridge, T: 617 492 2327.*

Screen Scenes

Brattle Theater ❶ 4C & ❸
Classic, foreign, and independent films. *40 Brattle St, Harvard Sq, Cambridge, T: 617 876 6837, www.brattlefilm.org*

Coolidge Corner Cinema ❶ 4C
Art, first-run, independent films, and documentaries. Midnight shows. *290 Harvard St at Beacon St, Brookline, T: 617 734 2501, www.coolidge.org*

The newly renovated Shubert Theater

Harvard Film Archive ❶ 4C
Repertoire of 5,000 all-time filmic gems. *Carpenter Center for the Visual Arts, 24 Quincy St at Broadway, Cambridge, T: 617 495 4700, www.harvardfilmarchive.org*

Museum of Fine Arts (MFA) ❷ 5A
More than 450 screenings and five film festivals a year: from Chinese documentary to Icelandic comedy. *465 Huntington Ave at Museum St, T: 617 267 9300, www.mfa.org/film*

Theater

Most venues are clustered along Tremont St between the Boylston T stop and Mass Pike.

American Repertory Theater ❶ 4C
Acclaimed productions from classics to challenging new works. *Loeb Drama Center, 64 Brattle St, Cambridge, T: 617 547 8300, www.amrep.org*

Boston Center for the Arts ❷ 5D
Experimental theater with four companies in residence and an eclectic mix of touring troupes. *539 Tremont St at Clarendon St, T: 617 426 5000.*

Colonial Theater ❷ 4E
A 1900 auditorium for off- and on-Broadway shows. *106 Boylston St at Tremont, T: 866 523 7469, www.broadwayinboston.com*

Huntington Theatre Company (University Theater) ❷ 5B
Vibrant program of new American plays. Is due to expand into two new venues. *264 Huntington Ave at Mass Ave, T: 617 266 0800, www.huntingtontheatre.org*

Bald & Blue
Founded on a sidewalk in the 1980s, the Blue Man Group is a dazzling, multi-sensory act exploring art and paint via a troupe of bald and blue-faced performers. See their crazy antics at the Charles Playhouse (❷5E), *74 Warrenton St, T: 617 931 2787, www.blueman.com*

Red Sox ticket office at Fenway Park

Lyric Stage ❷ 4D
Small, affordable off-Broadway productions. *140 Clarendon St at Copley Sq, T: 617 585 5678, www.lyricstage.com*

Sport

Baseball

The Red Sox are a local obsession (*see p.6*), and their exploits are followed with a passion bordering on the pathological. Good tickets are few and far between but they can be found, especially for day games and matches early in the season. Go to the box office rather than trying to buy tickets by phone.

Boston Red Sox ❷ 4A
4 Yawkey Way, Fenway Park, tickets T: 877 733 7699, www.redsox.com

Basketball

The Celtics are on the up. Tickets are easier to find than for the Red Sox.

Celtics ❷ 2G
FleetCenter, 1 Causeway St at North Station, North End, T: 800 4622 849, www.fleetcenter.com, www.celtics.com

Bike, Hike, Blade, & Board

Top biking and blading spots include all 18 miles of the **Charles River Esplanade** (❷ 3A-2E), **Memorial Drive** (❷ 2A-1E) on the Cambridge side of the Charles, and the **Minuteman Commuter Bikeway**, a 12-ft wide, 10-mile cycle path from Cambridge to Bedford (*T: 617 275 1111*). Hikers can take the **Green Mountains Long Trail** (off map) from Waterbury through Vermont to Canada (*T: 802 244 7037*).

Beacon Hill Skate Shop ❷ 5E
135 S Charles St at Oak St, I: 61 / 482 7400.

Back Bay Bikes & Boards ❷ 4B
336 Commonwealth Ave at Mass Ave, T: 617 247 2336.

Bowling

Unique to New England, 'candlepin' bowling is an elegant variation on the usual game, using narrower pins and lighter balls (around 2.5 lbs).

Lanes & Games ❶ 4C
34 candlepin and 20 ten-pin bowling lanes, complete with a restaurant

The Minuteman Commuter Bikeway

and fluorescent walls. *195 Concord Tpke, Somerville, T: 617 876 5533, www.lanesgames.com*

Milky Way Lounge & Lanes ❶6C
Illuminated lanes, pizza, and bowling to reggae, house, and salsa, with a karaoke night. *Open till 12am daily. 403-405 Centre St, Jamaica Plain (Stonybrook T), T: 617 524 3740.*

Football

Patriots ❶7C
The Patriots are mighty popular since a magnificent Superbowl winning streak in 2001, 2003, and 2004: advanced planning is advised. *CMGI Field, 60 Washington St, Foxboro, T: 617 931 2222, www.patriots.com*

Ice Hockey

Bruins ❷2G
Booking ahead is essential to see the Bruins. *TD Banknorth Garden, Causeway St at North Station, North End, T: 617 931 2222, www.bostonbruins.com, www.tdbanknorthgarden.com*

Sailing on the Charles River

Sailing & Kayaking

Boston Harbor Sailing Club ❷4H
Rentals and instruction. *58 Batterymarch St at Rowes Wharf, T: 617 720 0049, www.bostonharborsailing.com*

Boston Sailing Center ❷3H
Sailing instruction and boat rentals, from a riverboat in North End. *54 Lewis Wharf at Atlantic Ave, T: 617 227 4198, www.bostonsailingcenter.com*

Community Boating ❷3E
Sailing, kayaking, and windsurfing on the Charles River from April-October: experience is essential. *21 David Mugar Way btw Hatch Shell & Longfellow Bridge, T: 617 523 1038, www.community-boating.org*

Skiing

Advances in snow-making technology have extended the ski season from early fall to late spring.

Killington Ski Resort Off map
New England's biggest ski destination, with seven mountains and an 'endless' artificial winter. *4763 Killington Rd, Killington, T: 800 734 9435, www.killington.com*

Stowe Mountain Resort Off map
Some of the fastest, most exciting trails in New England, with night skis and a mountain-top chapel for weddings. *5781 Mountain Rd, Stowe, T: 802 253 3000, www.stowe.com*

Late night at the Milky Way Lounge

boston places to eat

Succulent seafood, fresh New England produce, and plenty of culinary wizardry are the staple ingredients of Boston's thriving restaurants. There's the chance to sample the essence of traditional Yankee fare – boiled beef, pot roast, clambake, clam chowder, and the baked beans that earned the Bostonians their 'Beantown' moniker. For gastronomes, the choice extends from Italian, French, and Mediterranean *haute cuisine* to tastebud-tingling Cambodian, Vietnamese, Chinese, and African experiences. As for seafood, whether it's cod, sea bass, juicy bay scallops, mussels, steamers, soft-shelled crabs, or the mighty Maine lobster, Boston reigns forever as king.

taste it places to eat

Brunch Time

Bob's Southern Bistro $$ ❷6B
Soul food like mamma made it – chitterlings, 'glorifried' chicken, and collard greens, all served up in an elegant South End bistro, with a Sunday jazz brunch showcasing musicians from nearby Berklee College. *604 Columbus Ave at Mass Ave, T: 617 536 6204.*

East Coast Grill & Raw Bar $$$ ❶4C
All manner of seafood and grilled meats, cooked up with a flamboyant Latin-American twist, plus a DIY Bloody Mary bar for a quick pick-me-up (see p.43). *1271 Cambridge St at Prospect St, T: 617 491 6568.*

Café Fleuri ❷4G & ❹
Book ahead for Boston's ultimate Sunday brunch, in The Langham Hotel and featuring hot main courses, a carvery, creperie, desserts galore, and jazz – expensive but well worth it. *The Langham, 250 Franklin St at Oliver St, T: 617 956 8751*

Caffè Vittoria, an old Boston favorite

Henrietta's Table $$$ ❶4C
The perfect Sunday brunch – unlimited portions of the freshest farm produce (see p.42) – but also good for breakfast, lunch, or dinner any other day of the week.*Charles Hotel, 1 Bennett St, Cambridge, T: 617 661 5005.*

Caffè Vittoria $ ❷3H
North End's oldest cafe, with espresso, cappuccino, pastries, and desserts to die for. *290-296 Hanover St at Prince St, T: 617 227 7607.*

Cheap Eats

Addis Red Sea $$ ❷5D
Spicy and genuine Ethiopian specialties. *544 Tremont St btw Clarendon & E Berkeley Sts, T: 617 426 8727.*

El Pelon Taqueria $ ❷4A
Authentic Mexican cuisine, very good value and very delicious. *92 Peterborough St at Boylston St, T: 617 262 9090.*

King Fung Garden $ ❷ 5F

Tiny and uninspiring at first glance, but well worth visiting for fabulous Shangdong province family banquets: scallion pancakes, pot stickers, and delectable dim sum; call ahead for the Peking Duck. *74 Kneeland St btw Hudson & Tyler Sts, T: 617 357 5262.*

No Name $$ ❷ 6H

With no frills, but worth seeking out for hot-from-the-dock clam rolls, fish chowder, beers, and bar-room sangfroid. *15 Fish Pier at Northern Ave, T: 617 423 2705.*

Pizzeria Regina $ ❷ 3G

Birthplace of the original North End thin-crust pizza – and a place of pilgrimage for sentimental Bostonians. *11 Thatcher St at N Margin St, T: 617 227 0765.*

> **Top Tipping Tips**
> The standard tip is 15-20 per cent (double the state tax), depending on the quality of the service. In bars, you should tip $1 a round.

Subtle surroundings at Aquitaine

Volle Nolle $ ❷ 3G

Delicious deli sandwiches, English muffins, and scores of tasty fillings; this unpretentious diner is a popular new kid on the block. *351 Hanover St, T: 617 523 0003.*

Chic & Sleek

Aquitaine $$$ ❷ 6D

Sophisticated ambiance and innovative bistro fare (steak frites, cassoulet, *coq au vin*, and bouillabaisse), in a stylish setting. *569 Tremont St at Union Park, T: 617 424 8577.*

Croma $$$ ❷ 4C

Upscale pizza and Mediterranean fare at this Newbury St haunt with large outdoor patio and gratifyingly endless wine-by-the glass options. *269 Newbury St, T: 617 247 3200, www.cromaboston.com*

Oleana $$$ ❶ 4C

Book ahead for this Cambridge hip spot, combining Mediterranean cooking with Middle Eastern accents; perfect for dining out *al fresco* in the summer. *134 Hampshire St btw Columbia & Prospect Sts, T: 617 661 0505.*

Rendezvous $$$ ❷ 4C

Acclaimed Boston chef Steve Johnson cooks up mouth-watering dishes

Scooper Dooper

Whether it's cucumber or chocolate-fudge brownie, Bostonians are the world's biggest ice cream eaters, devouring double the amount consumed by the rest of North America. Visit the annual Jimmy Fund Scooper Bowl, a three-day festival of ice cream held at City Hall Plaza in June, or head for Newbury St (❷4D) to Ben & Jerry's (*174 Newbury*), Herrell's (*224 Newbury*), Emack & Bolios (*290 Newbury*), and J P Licks (*352 Newbury – see pic above*). Over in Cambridge, Toscanini's (❷4C) supplies gourmet ice cream in green tea, saffron, burnt caramel, and even Guinness flavors (*1310 Mass Ave at Harvard Sq*).

inspired by the West Mediterranean. Pick a kitchen-view table. *502 Mass Ave, Cambridge T: 617 576 1900, www.rendezvouscentralsquare.com*

Tremont 647 $$$ ❷6C

This stylish restaurant has an award-winning Pajama Brunch on weekends and pet-friendly outdoor dining on Saturday afternoons. *645 Tremont St at W Brookline St, T: 617 266 4600.*

Classic Boston

Casa Romero $$$ ❷4C

This is a gem of a restaurant serving sophisticated, mouthwatering Mexican cuisine and outdoor dining. *30 Gloucester St btw Commonwealth Ave & Newbury St, T: 617 536 4341.*

Durgin Park $$ ❷3G

Touristy but fun, this popular Boston restaurant has been serving hearty Yankee fare since 1827: diners still feast family-style on the full range of local specialties, from prime rib, baked beans cooked with salt pork and molasses, Boston cream pie, and

classic Indian pudding. *5 Faneuil Hall Marketplace, 340 N Market St at Clinton St. T: 617 227 2038.*

Henrietta's Table $$$ ❶4C

A Cambridge institution: upscale New England meatloaf, chowders, pot pies, smoked pork chops in apple sauce, and roasts. It has a superb wine list, microbrews, and a legendary Sunday brunch (*see p.40*). *Charles Hotel, 1 Bennett St, Cambridge, T: 617 661 5005.*

Durgin Park serves up hearty local fare

Ethnic

Chau Chow City Restaurant $ ❷ 5F
On three stories: a Chinatown seafood and dim sum palace, perfect for a relaxing and long weekend lunch. *83 Essex St at Oxford, T: 617 338 8158.*

Elephant Walk $$$ ❶ 5C
Imaginative French-Cambodian culinary safari. *900 Beacon St at Park Drive, Brookline, T: 617 247 1500.*

Kashmir $$ ❷ 4C
The generous but subtly prepared curries at this Newbury St restaurant are the best in Boston: with a patio for outdoor dining and very popular lunchtime buffet. *279 Newbury St at Gloucester St, T: 617 536 1695.*

Expense Account

Azure $$$ ❷ 4C
Upscale hotel restaurant in the Lenox (see p.57) specializing in ocean-fresh exotic fish: sea bass, lobster, scallops, dab, and oysters galore. In addition to the fish, choose from rack of lamb, ribeye steak, and an extensive wine list. *Lenox Hotel, 65 Exeter St at Boylston St, T: 617 933 4800.*

Aujourd'hui $$$$ ❷ 4E
Restaurants don't get better, tastier, or more sophisticated than the stunning Aujourd'hui, spectacularily positioned in the Four Seasons Hotel (see p.57) with picture windows overlooking the Public Garden (see p.14). Bring a credit card made of strontium and gird your stomach muscles for the ultimate gastronomic splurge-out. *Four Seasons Hotel, 200 Boylston St btw Arlington & S Charles Sts, T: 617 351 2071.*

East Coast Grill & Raw Bar $$$$ ❶ 4C
A packed-out, atmospheric seafood and barbecue palace, run by Chris Thrill of the Grill Schlesinger, with great cocktails to match and a Bloody Mary Sunday brunch that's well worth leaving bed for (see p.40). *1271 Cambridge St at Prospect, Cambridge, T: 617 491 6568.*

Sophistication personified at Azure

The Federalist $$$$ ❷ 4F
Deliciously over-the-top dining in imposing surroundings (see p.58): grandiose nouvelle cuisine (lobster, Beef Wellington and so on) with a six-course tasting menu and a smart wine list. *Fifteen Beacon Hotel, 15 Beacon St at Bowdoin, T: 617 670 2515, www.xvbeacon.com*

Grill 23 & Bar $$$$ ❷4B

Boston's best and juiciest steaks: in comfy gentleman's club-style surroundings, with a cigar bar above. *161 Berkeley St at Stuart St & Columbus Ave, T: 617 542 2255.*

No 9 Park $$$$ ❷4F

Next to the State House: imaginative New American cuisine combined with a mixture of Italian flair and understatement by TV guru Barbara Lynch. *9 Park St at Beacon, T: 617 742 9991.*

Sorellina $$$$ ❷4D

No expense has been spared to make this restaurant a chic, stylish spot for its largely corporate clientele. Chef John Delpha crafts lip-smacking Italian dishes that melt in your mouth and portions are pleasingly generous. *1 Huntington Ave at Dartmouth St, T: 617 412 4600.*

Late Night

Dynasty $ ❷5F

Hong Kong seafood and dim sum. *Open till 4am. 33 Edinboro St btw Beach & Essex Sts, T: 617 350 7777.*

East Ocean City $$ ❷5F

A Chinatown stalwart for bona-fide 'fresh from the tank' seafood. *Open Sun-Thu till 3am, Fri-Sat till 4am, 25 Beach St btw Harrison Ave & Washington St, T: 617 542 2504.*

South Street Diner $ ❷5F

Open from 5pm till 5am during the week and 24hrs on weekends, this is the place to go for a very-early morning bite. *178 Kneeland St, T: 617 350 0028.*

Restaurant signs in Chinatown

Neighborhood Scenes

Carmen $$$ ② 3H

Sublimely inventive contemporary Italian cuisine in a cosy trattoria with seating for 30 and a bar. Reserve in advance. *33 North Sq at Prince St, T: 617 742 6421.*

Prezza $$$ ② 3G

One of the best *trattorie* in North End: inventive contemporary cooking by chef-owner Anthony Caturano. *24 Fleet St at Hanover, T: 617 227 1577.*

Sel de la Terre $$$ ② 4G

Close to the Aquarium (see p.12) and the Big Dig (see box, p.51) and providing nourishment and sanctuary in the form of robust Provençal bistro cuisine. Splash out on lunch at the bar, or choose picnic food from the boulangerie. *255 State St at Atlantic Ave, T: 617 720 1300.*

Sonsie $$$ ② 4B

Newbury St's preening and people-watching nirvana: strike up attitudes

Great cooking and great bar at Prezza

over coffee or mouth-watering New American-North Italian fusion food. *327 Newbury St btw Hereford & Mass Ave, T: 617 351 2500.*

Stephanie's on Newbury $$$ ② 4C

Deluxe, upmarket New American comfort food with prices to match. *190 Newbury St at Exeter, T: 617 236 0990.*

Romantic

L'Espalier $$$$ ② 4C

Elegant, expensive, and romantic; a beautiful Back Bay brownstone is the venue for memorable cooking by chef-owner Frank McClelland. *30 Gloucester St, T: 617 262 3023.*

Seafood

Legal Sea Foods $$-$$$ ② 4F

Flagship of the popular and ultra-reliable Boston chain: superb-quality clam chowder, lobster, and fritters, at reasonable prices. *26 Park Plaza at Park Sq, T: 617 426 4444, www.legalseafoods.com*
The façade of Legal Sea Foods

Fruits of the Sea

The icy waters around New England's coast are home to some of the world's finest seafood: native delicacies to savor include *scrod* (small cod or haddock), blue point oysters from around Cape Cod and Nantucket, and bay scallops. There are mouth-watering soft-shell crabs (only available in July), Maine lobster (or *homarus americanus*), and cherrystone and quahog clams, fried or stewed with potatoes, milk, and herbs to make classic Boston *chowder*.

Union Oyster House $$-$$$ ❷3G

Dating from 1826, this claims to be the oldest restaurant in continuous operation in the US. There is an old-fashioned tavern atmosphere complete with lobster pond, semi-circular raw bar, darkwood walls, and whitewashed booths (check out #18, where JFK sat on Sunday mornings). Best for blue point oysters, grilled or raw, followed by boiled lobster with drawn butter. *41 Union St at Faneuil Hall, T: 617 227 2750.*

Smiles all around in the Union Oyster House

Sushi

Ginza $$-$$$ ❷5F

Fresh from the boat, impeccable Tokyo-style sushi, sashimi, and tempura: in a fabulously atmospheric dining room. *Open Fri & Sat till 4am, 16 Hudson Street, T: 617 338 2261.*

Boston Bars

The Bristol Lounge ❷4E

The place to come for a Martini, this

That familiar sign in Cheers Bar

luxurious wood-panelled bar has a gentleman's club-like elegance and is handy for a pre- or post-theatre drink. *Four Seasons Hotel, 200 Boylston St, T: 617 338 4400.*

Cheers (aka The Bull & Finch) ❷ 4E

Don't count on them knowing your name, but you can't visit Boston without raising a pint at The Bull & Finch. Decent burgers and dancing at the weekend. *84 Beacon St at Arlington St, T: 617 227 9605.*

Doyle's Cafe $$ ❶ 5C

A favorite watering hole for politicians, but even so it's worth visiting for the atmosphere and 19th century boothed interior. Try classic chowder, giant burgers, or ribs. *3484 Washington St at Williams, Jamaica Plain, T: 617 524 2345.*

Les Zygomates ❷ 5F

A sophisticated wine-bar-bistro, offering a choice of 40 wines, including home-grown New England sparkling. There is live jazz, affordable but elegant bistro food, and wine tastings (6pm & 8pm Tue). *129 South St at Kneeland, T: 617 542 5108.*

Top of the Hub

For views, cocktails, and chocolate martinis, try the Prudential Center's Top of the Hub (❷4C), 52 stories high, with live jazz nightly. *Prudential Center, 800 Boylston St, T: 617 536 1775, www.selectrestaurants.com*

Doyle's Cafe – worth the journey

boston practical information

Small, compact, and bounded on three sides by riverbank and bay, Boston is dream terrain for the pedestrian. Most of the big sights are clustered in the historic center; negotiating the labyrinth of 18th-century streets can be confusing at times, but fortunately there's the 2.5-mile Freedom Trail to lead the way (stray from the red-brick path and you're liable to get lost, but then few cities in the world could be nicer to get lost in). Boston's big museums, universities, and cultural institutions are spread out, but all are easily accessible via an efficient and cheap public transportation system that connects every corner of the city via bus, ferry, and the oldest subway system in the nation.

know it practical information

Tourist Information

Boston Common Visitor Information Center ❷ 4F

Information on hotels, restaurants, shops, sights, museums, travel, sightseeing, and the Freedom Trail. *Open Mon-Sat 8.30am-5pm, Sun 10am-6pm, Boston Common & Tremont St, T: 888 733 2678, www.bostonusa.com*

Prudential Center Visitor Information Desk ❷ 5C

Information on Greater Boston, Massachusetts, and New England. *Open Mon-Sat 9am-6pm, Sun 10am-6pm.*

Boston Common Visitor Information Center

Arriving by Air

With heightened security post 9/11, all passengers should bring photo ID and allow two hours check-in time for domestic flights or three hours for international departures.

Logan International Airport ❶ 4E

Only two miles outside the city center, with five terminals (A-E) serving 40 airlines. *T: 617 428 2800, www.massport.com*

Transportation to and from the Airport

Free buses take arrivals to the **Airport T** (*see p.53*); from here it's a 10-15 minute ride by Blue Line T to Government Center or State Station near Faneuil Hall (❷4G). For sea-air, take the **MBTA Harbor Express** to Long Wharf (❷4H); the boat takes 7 minutes, $10, T: 617 222 6999. A 15-minute courtesy bus service connects Logan Dock to all airport terminals. *Mon-Sat 7am-10pm, Sun 7am-8pm.* **City Water Taxis** drop off at the World Trade Center (❻6H)

ATM at Bank of America

and Long Wharf (❷4H) for $10, and North Station (❷2G) and Charlestown (❶1G) for $20, T: 617 422 0392. Land taxis are available 24/7 at a metered rate starting at $1.75 and 30 cents each extra 1/8 mile. **A range of bus operators** run shuttles between Logan and South Station (❶5G), picking up at terminals B, C, & E, every 15-30 minutes in peak hours. *Logan Airport Hotline, T: 800 235 6426.*

Airport Handicap Van

Free transport between terminals and all airport locations for persons with disabilities. *T: 617 561 1769.*

Banks

Hours are Mon-Fri 9am-5pm, with some banks open 9am-12pm Sat. Most restaurants and stores take cash, travelers' checks, and plastic: ATMs are ubiquitous.

Changing Money

Bank of America

Foreign currency can be ordered over the phone or on their website. T: 888 660 0130, bankofamerica.com

Travelex

Branches in Terminal C and E of Logan Airport. T: 617 567 2153, www.travelex.com

Western Union ❷4F

At five locations including 144 Tremont St, T: 617 357 8021, www.westernunion.com

Car Hire

Avis ❶4E

Logan Airport and three locations in

The Big Dig

Costing $14 billion (seven times the estimate) and responsible for two decades of epic traffic jams, the Big Dig is the most costly public works project in US history. So far, the elevated Central Artery – an eyesore inflicted on the city in the 1950s – has been demolished and replaced with a 10-lane underground expressway, liberating 150 acres of land for parkland and redevelopment. For virtual tours of the dig see www.masspike.com/bigdig

---

the heart of Boston. Open 24 hours. T: 617 561 3500, www.avis.com

Hertz ❶4E, ❷5D, ❷4F

Seven branches including Logan Airport and 30 Park Plaza. T: 617 569 7272, www.hertz.com

Thrifty Car Rental ❷4E

Rentals from various locations in the

Boston area; one mile from Logan Airport (see left). T: 800 847 4389, www.thrifty.com

Driving in Boston

Costing $14.6 billion and responsible for two decades of epic traffic jams, the Big Dig (see left) has been the most costly public works project in US history. By late-2005 the elevated Central Artery had been demolished and replaced with a 10-lane underground expressway.

Car Parking

Interpark ❶4G

Parking garage a block from Faneuil Hall. 75 State St, T: 617 973 6760.

Cybercafés

Boston Public Library ❷4C

Has free terminals providing online access to all (see box, p.13). Copley Sq.

Trident Booksellers & Café ❶4D

This bookstore-and-café combo has

free wifi so you can bring your laptop, guzzle coffee and cake, and leave with the latest bestseller. *338 Newbury St T: 617 267 8688.*

Cycling

Boston is a small city, and you can cover a lot of ground in a short time. Top biking haunts include **Charles River Esplanade** and the **Minuteman Commuter Bikeway** from Cambridge to Bedford *(see p.36)*.

Disabled Access

Access is good for an American city; the terrain is mainly flat, and sidewalk curb-cuts are plentiful. The majority of T stations on the Blue, Red, and Orange Lines are wheelchair accessible, *see 'Boston Transit Map (❺)*; most buses kneel and some taxis have wheelchair lifts. For those who are unable to use general transport, the **MBTA** *(see right)* offers a lift-equipped van program called The Ride *(T: 617 222 5123).*

Massachusetts Office on Disability
Information on accessibility to more than 200 museums, theaters, and movie-houses. *T: 617 727 7440, www.mass.gov/mod*

MBTA Office for Transportation Access ❷ 5D
Reduced fares on public transport. Back Bay Station: *T: 617 222 5976* or *T: 800 543 8287, www.mbta.com*

VSA ❷ 4E
Info on museum and theater access. *2 Boylston St at Tremont St, T: 617 350 7713, www.vsamass.org*

Emergencies

Police, Ambulance, & Fire, *T: 911.*

CVS ❷ 4D
24-Hour pharmacy. *587 Boylston St, T: 617 437 8414.*

Massachusetts General Hospital ❷ 2E
55 Fruit St at Cambridge, T: 617 726 2000, www.mgh.harvard.edu

CVS is a 24-hour pharmacy

Tufts New England Medical Center ❷ 5F
750 Washington St at Kneeland, T: 617 636 5000, www.nemc.org

Lost & Found

Logan Aiport Lost & Found ❶ 4E
T: 617 561 1714.

MBTA Commuter Rail
North Station Lost & Found, T: 617 222 3600.

South Station Lost & Found ❷ 5G
T: 617 222 8120.

Subway & Bus Lost Property
T: 617 222 5000.

Mail

US letters cost 39¢ and postcards 24¢. Overseas letters are 84¢ and postcards cost 75¢ (63/55¢ Canada & Mexico). Stamps are sold at hotels, supermarkets, and stores as well as post offices (open 9am-5pm).

General Post Office ❷ 5G
Open 24 hours. Fort Point Station, 25 Dorchester Ave behind South Station, www.usps.com

Public Holidays

Jan 1	**New Year's Day**
3rd Mon Jan	**Martin Luther King Jr. Day**
3rd Mon Feb	**Presidents' Day**
Mar 17	**Evacuation Day & & St Patrick's Day**
3rd Mon Apr	**Patriots' Day**
Last Mon May	**Memorial Day**
Fri closest to Jun 17	**Bunker Hill Day**
Jul 4	**Independence Day**
1st Mon Sept	**Labor Day**
2nd Mon Oct	**Columbus Day**
4th Thu Nov	**Thanksgiving Day**
Nov 11	**Veterans' Day**
December 24	**Christmas Eve**
December 25	**Christmas Day**
December 31	**New Year's Eve**

Public Transportation

Providing good connections to every part of the metropolis, subways, buses, and commuter trains are operated by the MBTA (Massachusetts Bay Transportation Authority, *see left*), *T: 617 222 3200, www.mbta.com*

Buses

The bus system covers a more extensive network than the 'T' subway (*see right*) and costs a flat fare of 90¢, which is payable in exact change. Free transfers from bus to bus are valid up for up to two hours after issue of the ticket. Buses run daily from 5.30am-1am: detailed

The bus service is cheap and efficient

route maps are available from subway stations. *T: 617 222 5000.*

The T ❻

Dating from 1897, Boston's T is the oldest subway in America. It's fast and endearingly old-fashioned. It is also very cheap, with fares costing $1.25 (50¢ for under 12s, 35¢ for senior citizens) and $1.50-3 for zones further out. There are four main lines – **Red**, **Blue**, **Green**, and **Orange** – radiating outwards from the central points at Park St (❷1H), Government Center State (❸3G), and Downtown Crossing (❷4F). Trains are known as inbound or outbound, depending on whether they are heading to or away from

Park St T. *Open daily 5.45am-12.45am (Sun from 6am). Route and schedule info: www.mbta.com*

Taxis

Taxis can be hailed on major streets, or at stands outside hotels, train stations, and in Harvard Sq; metered fares start at $1.75. They are easy to find in the daytime, but are scarcer after 1am when the subway closes. **Town Taxi**: *T: 617 536 5000.*

Trains

Boston has three main central stations: South Station (**5**5G), North Station (**2**2G), and Back Bay (**5**5D), with MBTA commuter connections as far as Rockport, Providence, and Plymouth. Amtrak connections go to New York and Washington DC. Amtrak: *T: 800 872 7245, www.amtrak.com*

Telephones

Area code for the region: *857.* Code for the metropolitan area: *617.*

Local calls: *617 + seven digit number.* Calls to other area codes: *1+ the area code.* International calls: *011 + country code.* You can dial long distance and international calls directly from any pay phone using credit cards, cash, or low-cost phone cards sold at stores and newsstands.

Directory Assistance
www.superpages.com

Call Collect
Dial *0* and ask to make a collect call.

Signs outside a subway (T) station

New England Aquarium catamaran

Tours

Amphibious Landing Vehicle Duck Tours ❷4C
See box, p.5.

Old Town Trolley Tours
Hop-on, hop-off tours on ersatz trolley buses: 100-minute tours of the historic city, also specialty tours.
T: 617 269 7010,
www.historictours.com

Bike Tours

Boston Bike Tours ❷4F
Two-hour, low-impact jaunts through

the city, plus four-hour Sunday
Feature Tours. Bikes for all ages and
skills to hire. T: 617 350 0358,
www.bostonbiketours.com

Bus Tours

Innovation Odyssey ❷ 4G
Fascinating two-hour excursion of
sites connected to Boston's great
inventors. T: 617 574 5950,
www.innovationodyssey.com

MFA Architecture Tours ❷ 5A
Guided bus tours of architecture in
Beacon Hill and Back Bay. Prices from
$25. 465 Huntington Ave at Museum
St, T: 617 369 3395, www.mfa.org

Harbor Cruises

Boston Harbor Cruises ❷ 4H
Narrated tours, sunset, whale
watching. 1 Long Wharf, T: 617 227
4321, www.bostonharborcruises.com

Boston Steamship Co ❷ 4H
Moonlit cruises on replica steamships.
60 Rowes Wharf at Boston Harbor
Hotel, T: 617 542 8000,
www.massbaylines.com

Charles Riverboat Co ❷ D2 & 5H
Sunset cruises by paddleboat up
the Charles River Basin or Boston
Harbor, from $9.
T: 617 621 3001,
www.charlesriverboat.com

Liberty Fleet Tall Ship Adventures ❷ 4H
Sail round Boston Harbor Islands in a
replica 19th-century clipper: noon,
sunset, and Sunday brunch (Jun–Sep).
67 Long Wharf, T: 617 742 0333,
www.libertyfleet.com

Spirit Cruises ❷ 6H
Lobster, sunset harbor cruises,
and dinner and dancing aboard
Spirit of Boston. 200 Seaport Blvd,
World Trade Center, T: 866 211 3807,
www.spiritcruises.com

Whale-watching Tours

New England Aquarium ❷ 4H
Whale-watching trips take
three to four hours, tickets $32.55.
Open Apr-Oct, New England
Aquarium (❷4H),
T: 617 973 5200, www.neaq.org

Amphibious 'duck' riding the streets

The T Visitor Pass
This travel ticket is available
online or at Logan Airport
(❷4E), Boston Common
Visitor Information Center
(❷4F, see p.50), and the
Prudential Center (❷4C).
The T Visitor Passport gives
unlimited travel on subways,
buses, and inner-harbor
ferries for $7.50 (one day of
travel), $18 (three days of
travel), or $35 (seven days
of travel). www.mbta.com

directory

For locals as well as newcomers, this Boston directory has everything you need to get the best out of the city, from forthcoming exhibitions and annual events to finding the best hotels in all categories. There are suggestions for additional places of interest to visit not included in earlier chapters, and ideas for entertaining the kids. You'll also find a page of further reading, listings of popular websites, entertainment magazines, and local newspapers as well as a special feature on how to understand the Bostonians and speak their lingo.

Key to Icons

Hotels

Room Service	@ Business Centre
Restaurant	Health Centre
Fully Licensed Bar	Air Conditioning
En-suite Bathroom	P Parking

Museums

Toilets	
Disabled Facilities	
Refreshments	
Free Admission	
Guided Tours	

Places to Stay

Hotels in Boston veer between the affordable and the stratospheric, with a limited choice in between. The smartest are clustered around Back Bay, Downtown, and Beacon Hill; for a more economical experience try European-style guest houses in South End and Back Bay. During commencement and graduation – Sep, May, and Jun – accommodation is especially sparse.

Boston Brahmin

The Charles $$$$ ❶4C

Cambridge bastion of good taste, clean lines, elegant minimalism, and 19th-century American quilts: with sweeping views of the Charles River,

Price Guide Per Room

$ budget (under $120)
$$ moderate ($120-215)
$$$ expensive ($215-350)
$$$$ deluxe ($350 +)

a cutting-edge restaurant called Henrietta's Table (see p.43), and the Regattabar (see p.33). *1 Bennett St off Harvard Sq, T: 617 864 1200, www.charleshotel.com*

Fairmont Copley Plaza $$$ 2 4D

Boston's wonderfully old-fashioned Grande Dame of hotels dates back to 1912. Don't miss the Oak Room restaurant. *138 St James' Ave, Copley Sq, T: 617 267 5300, www.fairmont.com*

Four Seasons $$$$ 2 4E

At the pinnacle of perfection: deluxe rooms, many overlooking the Public Garden (see p.14), one of the city's top restaurants (Aujourd'hui, see p.43), and an awesome health spa. *200 Boylston St, T: 617 338 4400, www.fourseasons.com*

Ritz-Carlton $$$$ 2 4D

Boston's ultimate posh hotel – with

discreet, chic, and unspeakably swanky suites overlooking the Public Garden (see p.14), many with open wood fires. There's also a Ritz Carlton at Boston Common. *15 Arlington St at Newbury, T: 617 536 5700, www.ritzcarlton.com*

Upscale Glam

Boston Park Plaza $$$ 2 4E

With nearly 1,000 rooms, this hotel mingles old-fashioned panache with sheer 21st-century chic and glamor. *64 Arlington St at Newbury, T: 617 426 2000, www.bostonparkplaza.com*

Hotel Commonwealth $$$ 2 4A

Luxurious, comfortable rooms (150 in total) decorated in a classic style but equipped with modern amenities. Choose between views of Fenway Park, home of the Red Sox, and the historic Commonwealth Avenue. *500 Commonwealth Ave, T: 617 933 5000, www.hotelcommonwealth.com*

Lenox $$$ 2 4C

Charming old-world hotel: graceful decor and all conveniences. Most rooms have fireplaces. *710 Boylston St at Copley Sq, T: 617 536 5300, www.lenoxhotel.com*

Business Haven

Boston Harbor Hotel $$$$ 2 4H

Ultramodern hotel with a waterfront position, marina, pool, panoramic views, and a top-notch restaurant. *70 Rowes Wharf, T: 617 439 7000, www.bhh.com*

Seaport Hotel $$$$ ❷6H

The ultimate business hotel, close to the World Trade Center, with superb facilities. *One Seaport Lane at World Trade Center, T: 617 385 4000, www.seaporthotel.com*

Boutique Clique

Beacon Hill Hotel $$$ ❷3E

Twelve rooms in a magnificent 1830s townhouse, plus the Beacon Hill Bistro. *25 Charles St at Chestnut, T: 617 723 7575, www.beaconhillhotel.com*

Charles Street Inn $$$ ❷3E

Literary-themed luxury rooms with original fireplaces. *94 Charles St, T: 617 314 8900, www.charlesstreetinn.com*

Fifteen Beacon $$$$ ❷4F

Boston's swankiest boutique hotel with great dining at The Federalist (*see p.44*). *15 Beacon St at Bowdoin, T: 617 670 1500, www.xvbeacon.com*

Gryphon House $$ ❷3A

Quirky Back Bay gem with only eight rooms, all with tasteful decor and Internet connections. *9 Bay State Rd at Beacon St, T: 617 375 9003, www.gryphonhouseboston.com*

Hotel 140 $$ ❷5D

Attractive, contemporary rooms, hi-tech convenience and Back Bay on your doorstep: a real find. *140 Clarendon St, T: 617 585 5600, www.hotel140.com*

Jury's Boston $$$ ❷5D

Set in the city's old police HQ: spacious bathrooms, well-designed furniture, and a great location make this hotel a winner. *350 Stuart St, T: 617 266 7200, bostonhotels.jurysdoyle.com*

Value For Money

John Jeffries House $-$$ ❷3E

Modest but excellent Victorian-style hotel with small, well-appointed rooms, most with views of Charles River. *14 David Mugar Way at Charles St, T: 617 367 1866, www.johnjeffrieshouse.com*

Newbury Guest House $-$$ ❷4C

Three brownstones joined together with 32 bay-windowed quiet rooms. *261 Newbury St btw Gloucester & Fairfield Sts, T: 800 437 7668, www.hagopianhotels.com/ngh*

Budget

Chandler Inn $-$$ ❷5D

Friendly and high-decibel hotel in South End: mainly gay but welcoming straight guests. *26 Chandler St at Berkeley St, T: 617 482 3450, www.chandlerinn.com*

Midtown Hotel $-$$ **2** 5C

Unassuming hotel in Back Bay with excellent facilities. *220 Huntington Ave at Exeter St, T: 617 262 1000, www.midtownhotel.com*

Oasis Guest House $-$$ **2** 5B

Friendly, old-fashioned guest house with 16 comfortable rooms, guest kitchen, and outdoor deck. *22 Edgerly Rd & Westland Ave, T: 617 267 2262, www.oasisgh.com*

More Sights

Boston Center for the Arts **2** 5D

Includes theaters, art studios, and a small gallery. *539 Tremont St at Clarendon St, T: 617 426 2787, www.bcaonline.org*

Boston Tea Party Ship **2** 5G

Due to reopen spring 2007 after a fire. *Congress St Bridge, T: 617 338 1773, www.bostonteapartyship.com*

Bunker Hill Monument **2** 1G

Obelisk with steps to the memorial of the battle of Bunker Hill due to reopen in late 2006 with a new museum on site from mid-2007. *Monument Sq, Breed's Hill, Charlestown, T: 617 242 5642, www.nps.gov/bost*

Harrison Gray Otis House **2** 3F

Designed in 1796 by Charles Bulfinch (see p.10) in Federal style, with an opulent interior. *Tours: Wed-Sun 11am-4.30pm. 141 Cambridge St at Staniford St, T: 617 227 3956, www.historicnewengland.org*

Larz Anderson Auto Museum **1** 5C

Antique autos and cycles. *Larz Anderson Park, 15 Newton St, Brookline, T: 617 522 6547, www.mot.org*

Try a B&B

Mid-range accommodation is in short supply, so try the following: Bed & Breakfast Agency of Boston, with historic private homes in downtown, T: 617 720 3540, *www.boston-bnbagency.com*; Bed & Breakfast Associates Bay Colony, with 150 B&Bs from homestays to well-furnished apartments, T: 888 486 6018, www.bnbboston.com

Museum of Afro-American History **2** 3F

Interpretative exhibits and guided tours along the Black Heritage Trail (see box, p.14). *8 Smith Crt off 46 Joy St, T: 617 742 5415, www.afroammusem.org*

MIT Museum **2** 1B

Fascinating science and technology showcase. *265 Mass Ave at Windsor,*

T: 617 253 4444,
http://web.mit.edu/museum

Old North Church ❷ 2H

Exquisite Georgian church (see p.13): hourly guided tours from June to October, T: 617 523 4848 for reservations. 193 Salem St at Hull, T: 617 523 6676, www.oldnorth.com

Old South Meeting House ❷ 4G

Meeting-house where 5,000 angry colonists set off to the Boston Tea Party in 1773. 310 Washington St, T: 617 482 6439

Worcester Art Museum Off map

Massive art collection spanning 50 centuries. 55 Salisbury St, Worcester, T: 508 799 4406, www.worcesterart.org

Kids' Boston

Boston is great for entertaining kids. Essentials stops on their agenda should include Duck Tours (see p.5), the Public Garden (Swan Boat rides and the ducklings from Make Way for Ducklings, see pp.14 & 15), the Skywalk Observatory (see p.9), the Children's Museum (❷ 5G), the New England Aquarium (see p.12), cruises along Charles River (see p.53), and ice cream at J P Licks (see p.42). Info: www.boston-online.com/visitors/kids

Annual Events

January
Dance Across the City Day
(1st Sat): www.danceacrossthecity.org

February
Chinese New Year: parades, dragons, and fireworks, T: 617 536 4100.
Boston Wine Expo (2nd weekend): www.wine-expos.com/boston

March
Boston Massacre Re-enactment
(5 Mar): Old State House.
New England Spring Flower Show
(mid Mar): www.masshort.org

St Patrick's Day Parade (17 Mar): T: 617 536 4100.

April
Patriots' Day (3rd Mon).
Boston Marathon (3rd Mon): www.bostonmarathon.org

May
Lilac Sunday (3rd Sun): www.arboretum.harvard.edu

June
Dragon Boat Festival (early June): www.bostondragonboat.org
Lesbian & Gay Pride (1st week): T: 617 262 9405, www.bostonpride.org
Jimmy Fund Scooper Bowl (mid-Jun): eat ice cream for charity, www.jimmyfund.org
Cambridge River Festival (mid Jun): music, street performers, and dance.
Bunker Hill Day (3rd weekend): T: 617 242 5642.

July
Harborfest (1st week): www.bostonharborfest.com
Fourth of July: Pops 4 July Concert. T: 617 266 1492, www.bso.org

August
North End Italian Festas:
T: 617 536 4100.
Caribbean Carnival (mid Aug):
www.bostoncarnival.com

September
Boston Film Festival (2nd weekend):
www.bostonfilmfestival.org

October
Harvard Sq Oktoberfest:
www.harvardsquare.com
Head of the Charles Regatta
(2nd weekend): *www.hocr.org*

December
Tree Lighting (1st weekend):
ceremonial lighting of the Christmas
tree lights at Pru Center (*see 'Climb
to the Sky', p.9*) and Boston
Common (*see p.5*).
The Nutcracker: the Boston Ballet
presents the Tchaikovsky classic.
Wang Center (*see p.30*),
T: 617 695 6950,
www.bostonballet.org
First Night (31 Dec): city-wide arts
and entertainments party: parades,
music in churches, theaters, and

galleries, ice-sculpting on Copley Sq
and Boston Common, climaxing
with fireworks over Boston Harbor.
T: 617 542 1399, www.firstnight.org

Listings

Boston Globe
Boston's oldest broadsheet – owned
by the *New York Times*; good
coverage of work events, arts, sport,
theater, and entertainment, updated
daily at *www.boston.com*

The Phoenix
Alternative arts and entertainment
weekly, with politics, profiles, and
features, and with excellent arts,
restaurants, and shopping coverage,
www.thephoenix.com

Boston Herald
Timeless tabloid melange of noisy
headlines, crime stories, local gossip,
and sports. *www.bostonherald.com*

Bay Windows
Gay and lesbian weekly with listings
information, *www.baywindows.com*

Zagat Boston Restaurants
First-class restaurant guide available
in good book shops, *www.zagat.com*

Reading

The Bostonians, **Henry James.**
James' unflinching 1886 satire.

King's Handbook of Boston Harbor,
Moses King. Lavishly illustrated
reprint of the original 1888 guide.

All Souls: A Story of Southie, **Michael
Patrick MacDonald.** Intense and
haunting memoir of mobster
violence and childhood in the 1970s.

Web Sites

www.boston.com/ae/

www.boston-online.com

www.thephoenix.com

www.futureboston.org

speak it

The archetypical Bostonian noise – caricatured on T-shirts as a nasal "Pahk the cah in Harvihd Yahd" – emanates from white Irish-American South Boston (Southie). According to the stereotype, Bostonians habitually drop their "r's", saying "cahn't" instead of "can't" and "shuah" instead of "sure", with the renegade "r's" randomly cropping up elsewhere (as in "no idear") alongside various other lost consonants ("tawnic" instead of "tonic", "mayan" instead of "mine").

Greater Boston is racially diverse, and alongside traditional Irish, Italian, and Jewish enclaves, there are now African-American, Haitian, Ethiopian, Asian, South American, Middle Eastern, and Indian cultures. Together their influences are having an affect on the continual development of the local patois.

Athens of America – Boston absorbs over 200,000 students attending over 60 colleges a year.

The B's – The Bruins, pronounced "brooins" (see p.37).

Bahnie – pronounced "Barney" (derisive): pseudo-intellectual Harvard student.

Beantown – Bostonians abhor this out-of-towner's nickname.

Bosox – Boston Red Sox baseball team.

Bubbla – a water fountain.

The Cs – Boston Celtics basketball team (see p.36).

Chowderhead – a fool.

Comm Ave – Commonwealth Avenue.

Dot Ave – Dorchester Avenue.

Frappe – milkshake made of milk, ice cream, and syrup (pronounced "frap").

The Hub or **The Hub of the Solar System** – Boston, originally used by Oliver Wendell Holmes to refer to the State House.

Jimmies or **smoosh-ins** – little bits of chocolate or candy for sprinkling on ice creams.

JP – Jamaica Plain: a southern neighborhood.

Faneuil Hall – historic building and shopping mall pronounced "Fan-yull", "Fan-ull", or "Fan-you-al".

Mass Ave – Massachusetts Avenue.

Na-ah – no.

The Pike – Massachusetts Turnpike.

The Pit – entrance to Harvard Sq T, home to assorted dropouts.

The Pru – The Prudential Center

Quahogs – Native American name for hard-shelled clams ("ko-hogs").

Shawmut – anglicized Native American Indian name for Boston.

Shuah – all right, OK.

Spuckie – a sub or sandwich roll.

Succotash – a pale-colored porridge-like gruel made of corn, beans, meat, or fish.

The T – Boston's rapid transit system

Wicket – way beyond cool or bad.

Yaz – you, as in "catch yaz latah".

Yar – yes.

Written by Vanessa Letts and
Laetitia Clapton.

Pictures © Compass Maps
Ltd and Susannah Sayler,
Corbis, Stone, Image Bank,
Boston Common Visitor
Centre, Museum of Natural
History, Jon Arnold Images.
Cover Images: Alamy, Getty.

Whilst every effort has been
made to trace the
photography copyright
holders, we apologise for any
omissions. We would be
pleased to insert appropriate
credits in any future editions.

info@popoutmaps.com
www.popout-travel.com
© 2007 Compass Maps Ltd.

Patents Pending Worldwide.
popout™cityguide as well as
individual integrated
components including
popout™map and associated
products are the subject of
Patents Pending Worldwide

AA 3241

❸ A ONE-HOUR WALK AROUND HARVARD SQUARE

① **Harvard Yard** — Graduation ceremonies are held on this green each spring.
② **Widener Library** — 3.2 million volumes housed on over 5 miles of bookshelves.
③ **Carpenter Center** — Le Corbusier's 60's concrete and glass design.
④ **Memorial Church** — View war memorials inside this magnificent building.
⑤ **Harvard Hall** — (1776) Contains the college's first building.
⑥ **Massachusetts Hall** — Harvard's oldest standing building.
⑦ **Old Burying Ground** — Resting place of Revolutionary War soldiers as well as Harvard's early presidents.
⑧ **Christ Church** — Used as barracks during Revolutionary War.
⑨ **Dawes Island** — See the brass hoofprints from where William Dawes warned "The British are coming....."
⑩ **Washington Elm** — Here Gen. George Washington assembled his troops in 1775.
⑪ **Radcliffe Yard** — Wander in for some peace and quiet.
⑫ **Blacksmith House** — Once the home of Longfellow's "The Village Blacksmith"
⑬ **The Coop** — The Harvard Co-operative Society was formed in 1882 by students to combat high prices.